Under My Hat

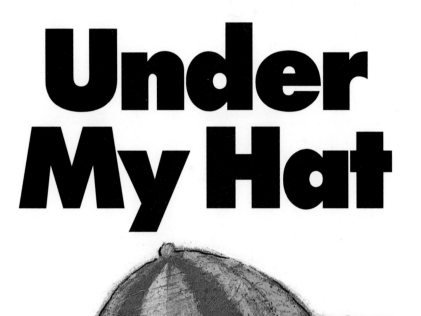

Titles in This Set

About the Cover

The artist Andrew Shachat painted the pictures on the
cover of this book. Mr. Shachat collects toys, especially tin
toys and robots. He says that he gets ideas for his pictures from
his collection.

ISBN 0-673-80011-3

Copyright © 1993
Scott, Foresman and Company, Glenview, Illinois
All Rights Reserved.
Printed in the United States of America.

Acknowledgments appear on page 128.

12345678910 VHJ 9998979695949392

Under My Hat

ScottForesman

A Division of HarperCollins*Publishers*

4

A Book to Share

Look at Me

5

My Favorite Things

Look at Me

So Can I

by Allan Ahlberg
and Colin McNaughton

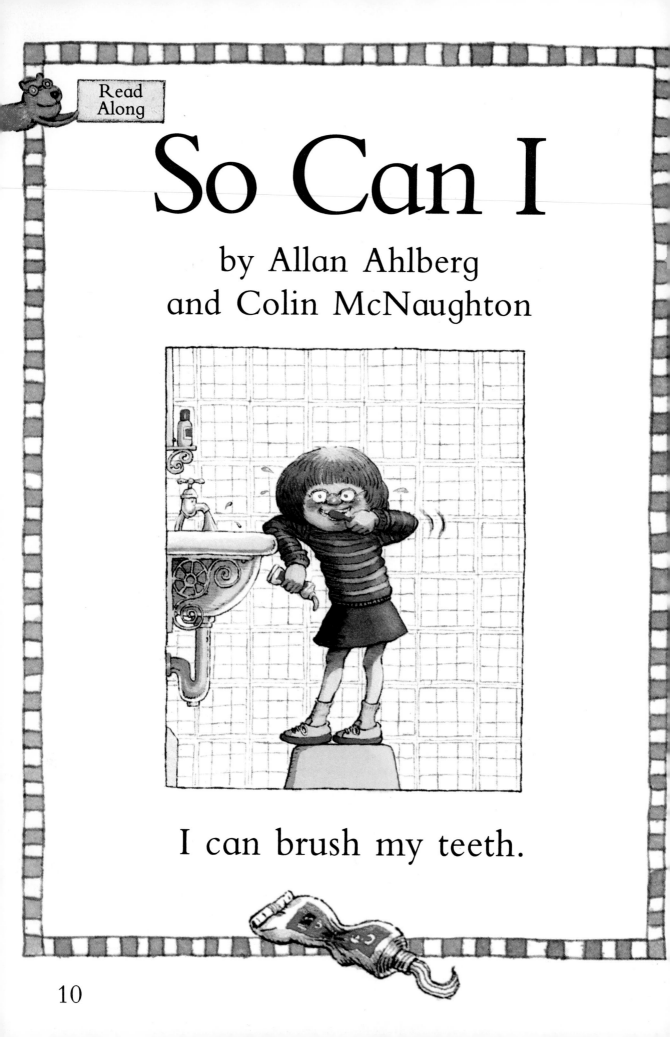

I can brush my teeth.

I can write my name.

I can read a book.

15

I can carry the groceries.

I can brush my teeth and
write my name and
read a book and
carry the groceries.

Big

by Dorothy Aldis

Now I can catch and throw a ball

And spell

Cat. Dog.

And Pig,

I have finished being small

And started

Being **Big.**

What Shall We Do When We All Go Out?

illustrations by Loreen Leedy

What shall we do when we all go out,
All go out, all go out,

What shall we do when we all go out,
When we all go out to play?

We will skate on our roller skates,

Roller skates, roller skates,

We will skate on our roller skates,

When we all go out to play.

We will ride our bicycles,

Bicycles, bicycles,

We will ride our bicycles,

When we all go out to play.

We will swing high and low,

High and low, high and low,

We will swing high and low,

When we all go out to play.

When I Count to One

illustrations by Ann Grifalconi

When I count to one

Do a dance with me

I say

Cha cha boom

Cha cha boom

That's what I say.

When I count to two

Do a dance with me

I say

Cha cha boom

Cha cha boom

That's what I say.

When I count to three
Do a dance with me

I say
Cha cha boom
Cha cha boom
That's what I say.

  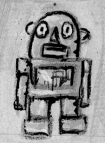 

My Favorite Things

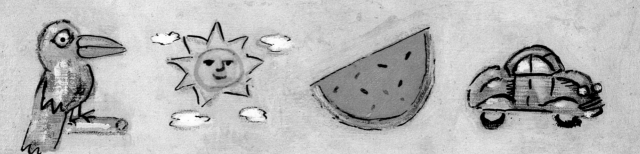

ONE GORILLA

by Atsuko Morozumi

Here is a list of things I love.

One gorilla.

Two butterflies among the flowers
and one gorilla.

Three parakeets in my house
and one gorilla.

43

Four squirrels in the woods
and one gorilla.

Five pandas in the snow
and one gorilla.

Six rabbits in a field
and one gorilla.

Seven frogs by the fence
and one gorilla.

Eight fish in the sea
and one gorilla.

Nine birds among the leaves
and one gorilla.

Ten cats in my garden
and one gorilla.

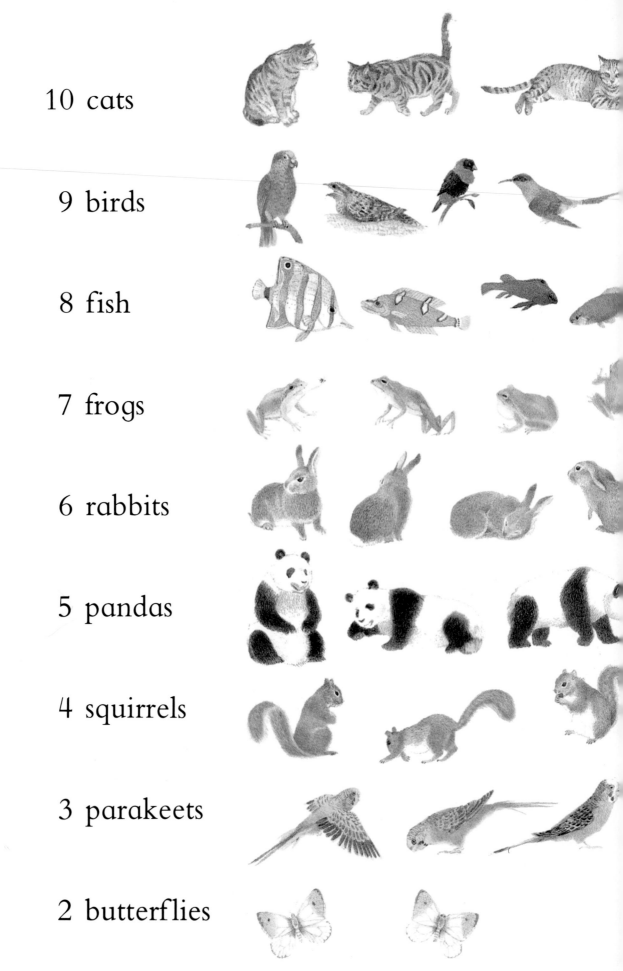

10 cats

9 birds

8 fish

7 frogs

6 rabbits

5 pandas

4 squirrels

3 parakeets

2 butterflies

But where is my gorilla?

Ah, there he is.

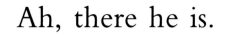

61

MY GORILLA

by Atsuko Morozumi

I used to live in London, England.

When I went to visit the London Zoo, I drew pictures of a very large gorilla who lived there. That gave me the idea for my book, <u>One Gorilla</u>.

To make all the other animals and things in my book look real, I drew from photographs and drawings.

I tried to hide the animals in my drawings. I used colors and many objects to make them hard to see.

Were you able to find them all?

Atsuko Morozumi

Little Fish

Little fish move in the water, swim, swim, swim.

Fly, fly, fly.

Little ones, little ones.

Fly, fly, fly.

Swim, swim, swim.

Los pececitos

Los pececitos van en el agua, nadan, nadan, nadan.

Vuelan, vuelan, vuelan.

Son chiquititos, chiquititos.

Vuelan, vuelan, vuelan.

Nadan, nadan, nadan.

65

Froggie, Froggie

Froggie, froggie.

Hoppity-hop!

When you get to the sea

You do not stop.

Plop!

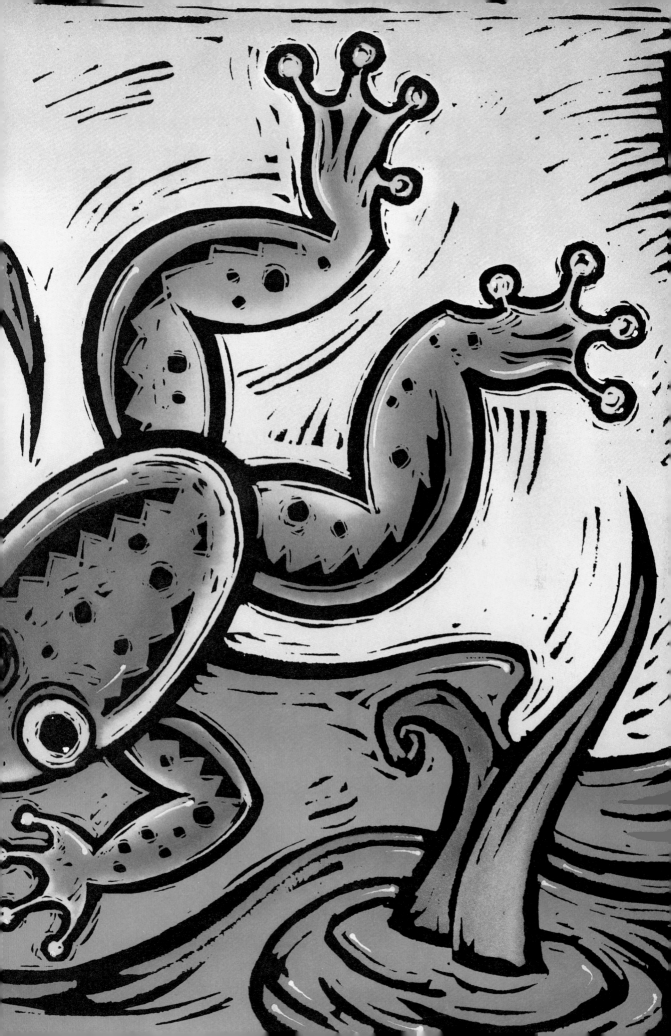

Mary Had a Little Lamb

by Sarah Josepha Hale

photo-illustrations by Bruce McMillan

M ary had a little lamb,

Its fleece was white as snow.

And everywhere that Mary went

The lamb was sure to go.

It followed her to school one day.

That was against the rule.

It made the children laugh and play

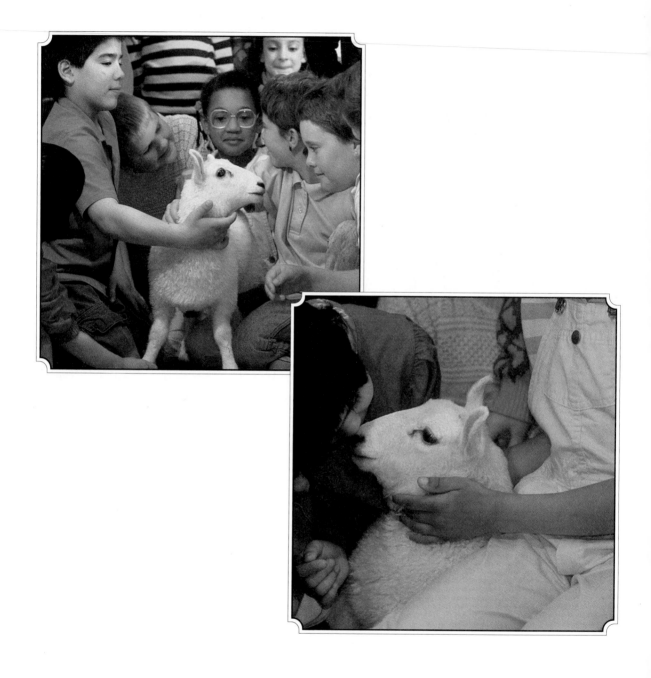

To see a lamb at school.

Taking Pictures of Mary and Her Lamb

by Bruce McMillan

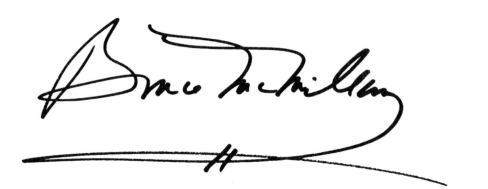

To take pictures for <u>Mary Had a Little Lamb</u>,
I needed someone to be Mary.
I found a pretty first-grade girl named
Sarah Jackson.

Second, I needed a lamb.
I found a frisky, young lamb named Argyle.

Photo: Benner McGee

Every day before I took any pictures,
Argyle got a bath. Why?
His fleece had to be "as white as snow."

I have a new sweater made from Argyle's wool.
Can you guess what color it is?

One Little Lamb

by Joan Knight

One little lamb put on records,

Two little lambs put on the light,

Three little lambs put the rug away,

Four little lambs got a fright,

Five little lambs toddled off to bed

And called to the others, "Goodnight!"

New Puppy

by Aileen Fisher

I can't *wait*

for school to be over,

can't *wait*

to rush down the street,

For I
have a new brown puppy
with funny white socks
for feet.

He's the wiggliest
bundle of wiggles
you ever
could hope to see.

I can't *wait* . . .
and I hope my puppy
is waiting as hard
for me.

OLD HAT NEW HAT

by Stan
and Jan
Berenstain

Old hat.

Old hat.

New hat.

New hat

New hat

New hat

New hat

Too big.

Too small.

Too flat.

Too tall.

Too loose.

Too tight.

Too heavy.

Too light.

Too red.   Too dotty.

Too blue.   Too spotty.

Too fancy.

Too frilly.

Too shiny.

Too silly.

Too
beady.

Too
bumpy.

Too
leafy.

Too
lumpy.

Too
holey.

Too
patchy.

106

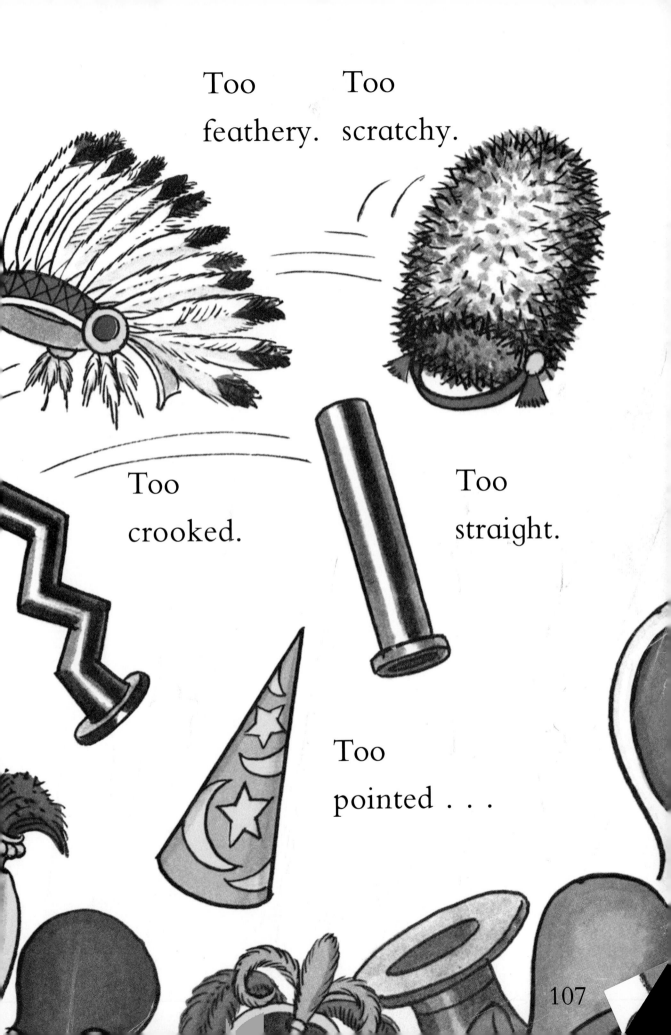

Too
feathery.

Too
scratchy.

Too
crooked.

Too
straight.

Too
pointed . . .

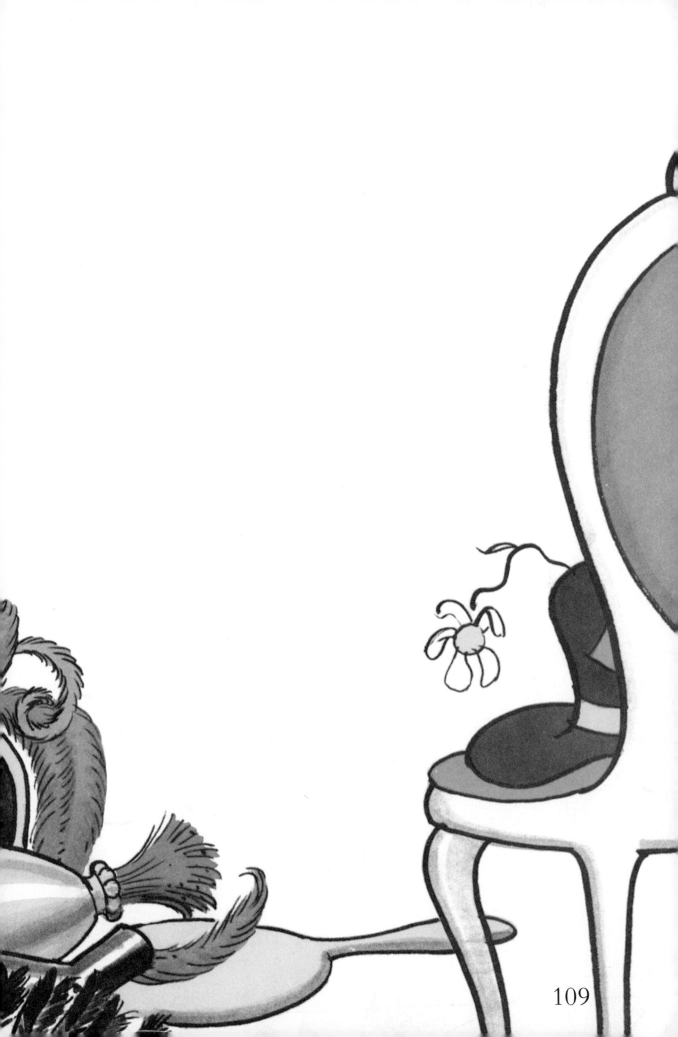

Just right!

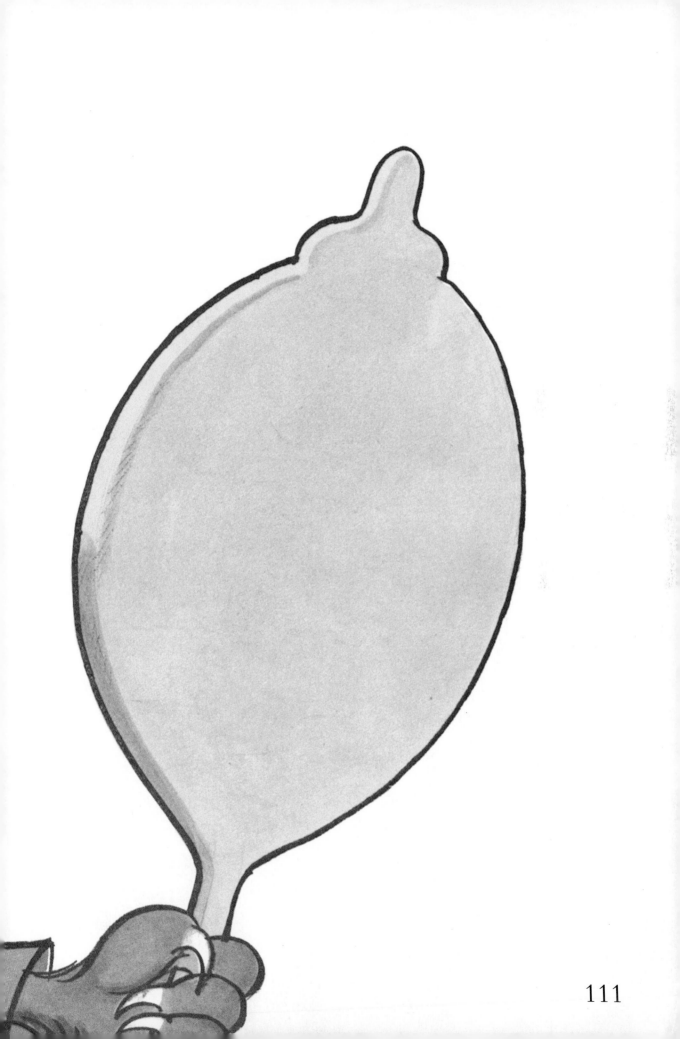

Just right.

Just right.

New hat.

Old hat.

OUR BOOK ABOUT HATS

by Stan and Jan Berenstain

We wrote and illustrated <u>Old Hat, New Hat</u> many years ago when our two sons were young children.

Both of our sons, Leo and Michael, loved hats. They had many different kinds of hats. So we decided to write and illustrate a Bear book about hats for our sons to enjoy.

Our sons now read <u>Old Hat, New Hat</u> to their young children, who also love hats.

Hats

by William Jay Smith

Round or square

Or tall or flat,

People love

To wear a hat.

119

Notice

by David McCord

I have a dog,

I had a cat.

I've got a frog

Inside my hat.

Books to Enjoy

It Looked Like Spilt Milk
by Charles Shaw

What a funny-looking thing!
Is it a bird? Is it a flower?
Read and think about what
each shape might be.

Fur
by Jan Mark
Illustrations by Charlotte Voake

Why would a cat want to look
for a hat? What do you think?

Things I Like
by Anthony Browne

Monkey likes to ride a bike.
Find out if he likes to do any
of your favorite things.

A Playhouse for Monster

by Virginia Mueller
Illustrations by Lynn Munsinger

Monster has his playhouse all
to himself. Why isn't he happy?

We Hide, You Seek

by Jose Aruego and Ariane Dewey

A rhinoceros plays hide and seek.
See which hiding place is best.

Everything Grows

by Raffi
Photo-illustrations by Bruce McMillan

Everything grows and grows.
Brothers, sisters, babies too.

Pictionary

Favorite Things To Do

roller-skate

race

FINISH

eat popcorn

swing

ride a bicycle

ad a book

throw a ball

jump rope

laugh

125

Opposites

short

long

many

full

empty

light

heavy

back

front

big

small

loose

tight

127

Acknowledgments

Text

Page 10: *So Can I* by Allan Ahlberg and Colin McNaughton. Text copyright © 1985 Allan Ahlberg. Illustrations copyright © 1985 Colin McNaughton. Published in the United Kingdom by Walker Books Limited. Reprinted by permission.

Page 20: "Big" by Dorothy Aldis. Reprinted by permission of G. P. Putnam's Sons from *All Together* by Dorothy Aldis, copyright © 1925–1928, 1934, 1939, 1952, copyright renewed 1953–1956, 1962, 1967 by Dorothy Aldis.

Page 22: "What Shall We Do When We All Go Out?" from *Sharon, Lois and Bram's Mother Goose.* Text and musical arrangement copyright © 1985 by Grand Trunk Music. By permission of Little, Brown and Company, in association with Joy Street Books and Douglas & McIntyre.

Page 30: "When I Count to One" from *Apples on a Stick* by Barbara Michels and Betty White, text copyright © 1983 by Barbara Michels and Betty White. Reprinted by permission of Coward-McCann, Inc.

Page 38: *One Gorilla* by Atsuko Morozumi. Text copyright © 1990 by Mathew Price. Illustrations copyright © 1990 by Atsuko Morozumi. Reprinted by permission of Mathew Price Ltd.

Page 62: "My Gorilla," by Atsuko Morozumi. Copyright © 1991 by Atsuko Morozumi.

Page 64: "Little Fish" from *Tortillitas Para Mama* selected and translated by Margo C. Griego, Betsy L. Bucks, Sharon S. Gilbert and Laurel H. Kimball. Copyright © 1981 by Margo Griego, Betsy Bucks, Sharon Gilbert and Laurel Kimball. Reprinted by permission of Henry Holt and Company, Inc.

Page 66: "Froggie, Froggie" from *Chinese Mother Goose Rhymes* selected and edited by Robert Wyndham, copyright © 1968 by Robert Wyndham. Reprinted by permission of Philomel Books.

Page 68: Photos from *Mary Had a Little Lamb* by Sara Josepha Hale copyright © 1990 by Bruce McMillan. All Rights Reserved. Reprinted by permission of Scholastic, Inc. Line drawing © 1990 by Bruce McMillan.

Page 80: "Taking Pictures of Mary and Her Lamb," by Bruce McMillan. Copyright © 1991 by Bruce McMillan.

Page 82: "One Little Lamb" from *Tickle-Toe Rhymes* by Joan Knight. Text copyright © 1989 by Joan Knight. Illustration copyright © 1989 by John Wallner. Reprinted by permission of the publisher, Orchard Books.

Page 84: "New Puppy" from *Feathered Ones and Furry* by Aileen Fisher. Text copyright © 1971 by Aileen Fisher. Reprinted by permission of HarperCollins Publishers.

Page 88: *Old Hat, New Hat* by Stan and Jan Berenstain. Copyright © 1970 by Stan and Jan Berenstain. Reprinted by permission of Random House, Inc.

Page 116: "Our Book About Hats," by Stan and Jan Berenstain. Copyright © 1991 by Stan and Jan Berenstain.

Page 118: "Hats" from *Laughing Time* by William Jay Smith. Copyright © 1989, 1990 by William Jay Smith. Reprinted by permission of Farrar, Straus and Giroux, Inc.

Page 120: "Notice" from *One at a Time* by David McCord. Copyright © 1952 by David McCord. By permission of Little, Brown and Company.

Artists

Illustrations owned and copyrighted by the illustrator.
Andrew Shachat, 1–9, 36–37, 120–127
Colin McNaughton, 10–19
Keiko Narahashi, 20–21
Loreen Leedy, 22–29
Ann Grifalconi, 30–35
Atsuko Morozumi, 38–63
David Diaz, 64–67
Bruce McMillan, 68
John Wallner, 82–83
Paul Meisel, 84–87
Stan and Jan Berenstain, 88–115
Marc Rosenthal, 118–119

Photographs

Page 63: Courtesy of Atsuko Morozumi
Pages 69–79: Bruce McMillan
Page 81: Benner McGee (Courtesy of Bruce McMillan)
Page 116: Courtesy of Stan and Jan Berenstain